good answers
to tough questions

About Stepfamilies

Written by Joy Berry

Copyright© Joy Berry, 2022
Originally Published, 1990

All rights are reserved.

No part of this book can be duplicated or used without the prior written permission of the copyright owner, except for the use of brief quotations from the book.

For inquiries or permission requests contact the publisher.

Published by Joy Berry Enterprises
www.joyberryenterprises.com

This book can give you some good answers to tough questions about
- terms that relate to stepfamilies,
- feelings stepchildren might experience,
- disadvantages of being part of a stepfamily,
- advantages of being part of a stepfamily, and
- recommended things for stepchildren to avoid.

## 4 — TERMS THAT RELATE TO STEPFAMILIES

Some parents are responsible for the physical birth of their children. These parents are called **biological parents**. They are also called **natural parents** or **birth parents**.

## TERMS THAT RELATE TO STEPFAMILIES — 5

Not all children live with their biological parents. Sometimes biological parents die or they are unable to take care of their children.

In either situation, the children might be adopted by other adults. When adults adopt children, they promise to take care of the children. Adults who adopt children are called *adoptive parents*.

## 6 — TERMS THAT RELATE TO STEPFAMILIES

Not all children live with biological or adoptive parents. Sometimes one parent dies, and the parent who is still alive marries another person.

Sometimes a parent divorces and marries someone else.

In either situation, a person who marries a parent with children becomes a *stepparent* to the children. A stepparent can also be called an *acquired parent* or a *surrogate parent*.

Children who have stepparents are called **stepchildren**. And families who have stepparents and stepchildren are called **stepfamilies**.

A stepfamily can also be called a **blended household**, **combination family**, **expanded family**, or **merged family**.

## 8 — TERMS THAT RELATE TO STEPFAMILIES

Children who live in the same stepfamily and do not have the same biological parent are called **stepbrothers** or **stepsisters**.

When a child's biological parent and stepparent have a baby together, the baby is the child's **halfbrother** or **halfsister**. And the child is the baby's halfbrother or halfsister.

## 10 — FEELINGS STEPCHILDREN MIGHT EXPERIENCE

Children who are members of stepfamilies often experience some uncomfortable feelings.

Some children feel **sad** over the loss of their original family. They feel sad that they cannot live with both of their biological parents in the same house.

## FEELINGS STEPCHILDREN MIGHT EXPERIENCE — 11

Some stepchildren feel *out of control*. They feel that they have no control over what is happening to them.

## FEELINGS STEPCHILDREN MIGHT EXPERIENCE

Some stepchildren feel **resentful**. They resent that they are expected to cooperate with decisions and plans that they did not want or make.

## FEELINGS STEPCHILDREN MIGHT EXPERIENCE — 13

Some stepchildren feel *angry*. They feel angry that things are not happening the way they want them to happen.

## 14 — FEELINGS STEPCHILDREN MIGHT EXPERIENCE

Some stepchildren feel *frustrated*. They feel frustrated that they have to start all over again and adjust to a new situation.

## FEELINGS STEPCHILDREN MIGHT EXPERIENCE — 15

Some stepchildren feel *afraid*. They fear that if and when they finally adjust to their new situation, things will change again. Then they will have to go through the difficulty of adjusting to yet another new situation.

**16 — FEELINGS STEPCHILDREN MIGHT EXPERIENCE**

Some stepchildren feel *jealous*. They feel jealous of the time and attention their biological parents give to their stepparents, stepbrothers, stepsisters, halfbrothers, or halfsisters.

**FEELINGS STEPCHILDREN MIGHT EXPERIENCE — 17**

Some stepchildren feel *insecure*. They feel that their stepparents do not love them and do not want them around. Thus, they feel unsure of what is going to happen to them.

## 18 — DISADVANTAGES OF BEING PART OF A STEPFAMILY

As in every situation, there are both disadvantages and advantages of being part of a stepfamily.

Some stepchildren do not like to share their biological parents' attention and affection with other stepfamily members.

**DISADVANTAGES OF BEING PART OF A STEPFAMILY — 19**

Some stepchildren do not like having a stepparent telling them what to do and what not to do.

I WOULD LIKE FOR YOU TO CLEAN YOUR ROOM BEFORE YOU GO TO YOUR FRIEND'S HOUSE, WENDY.

YOU'RE **NOT** MY MOTHER AND I DON'T NEED ANOTHER PERSON TELLING ME WHAT TO DO!

AND I SUPPOSE YOU WANT ME TO CLEAN MY LITTER BOX?

## DISADVANTAGES OF BEING PART OF A STEPFAMILY

Some stepchildren do not like having to share their living space or other things with stepfamily members.

**DISADVANTAGES OF BEING PART OF A STEPFAMILY — 21**

Some stepchildren do not like the additional noise, chaos, and confusion that happens when other people are added to a family.

## 22 — ADVANTAGES OF BEING PART OF A STEPFAMILY

In spite of the uncomfortable feelings and disadvantages, there are many advantages to being part of a stepfamily.

Parents who live in negative situations are usually unhappy. It is difficult for children to live with unhappy parents.

When these parents get out of their negative situations, they oftentimes become happier and more desirable to live with.

ADVANTAGES OF BEING PART OF A STEPFAMILY — 23

Single parents (parents who do not have a husband or wife) are often depressed because they feel lonely and overburdened with the responsibility of maintaining a household by themselves. It is not pleasant for children to live with parents who are depressed.

When these parents get a companion who will share the household responsibilities, they oftentimes stop being depressed. It becomes more pleasant for their children to live with them.

## 24 — ADVANTAGES OF BEING PART OF A STEPFAMILY

Sometimes it is better for children to live with two parents rather than one.

When one parent cannot or does not want to do something for a child, the other parent might be able or willing to do it.

## ADVANTAGES OF BEING PART OF A STEPFAMILY — 25

Additional people in a family can decrease the amount of work each person has to do. The more people there are in a family, the more people there are to share the work that needs to be done.

## 26 — ADVANTAGES OF BEING PART OF A STEPFAMILY

Additional people in a family can increase the amount of fun the family can have. There are more people to come up with interesting things to do. There are more people to play and have fun with.

## ADVANTAGES OF BEING PART OF A STEPFAMILY — 27

When people are added to a family, relatives are added as well. Having more relatives can result in more family get-togethers and more holiday celebrations together.

# RECOMMENDED THINGS FOR STEPCHILDREN TO AVOID

Stepchildren can help determine whether being part of a stepfamily will be a positive or negative experience. To make the experience a positive one, it is necessary to avoid doing negative things.

**Avoid doing things to destroy the relationship between your biological parent and your stepparent.**

Contributing to the breakdown of their relationship could cause you to feel very guilty. It could also cause them to feel resentful toward you.

**RECOMMENDED THINGS FOR STEPCHILDREN TO AVOID — 29**

**Avoid resenting the time that your biological parent spends with your stepparent or other members of your stepfamily.**

If your biological parent spent all of his or her time with you, both of you would most likely get tired of each other. This would put a strain on your relationship. Relationships do best when people spend some time together *and* some time apart from each other.

# 30 — RECOMMENDED THINGS FOR STEPCHILDREN TO AVOID

**Avoid involving your biological parent in disagreements between your stepparent and you.**

Adding a third person to a disagreement between two people only complicates things. When disagreements become complicated, they become difficult, if not impossible, to resolve. Unresolved disagreements lead to strained relationships in which everyone feels uncomfortable.

**Avoid becoming involved in disagreements between your biological parents and stepparents.**

The disagreements between your biological parents and stepparents are their problem, not yours. You only complicate matters when you become involved. It is best for you to refuse to take sides and insist that your parents resolve their disagreements without your participation.

# RECOMMENDED THINGS FOR STEPCHILDREN TO AVOID

**Avoid comparing your biological parents with your stepparents.**

Remember that every person is unique and has his or her own set of strengths and weaknesses.

If you expect any parent to be perfect, you will most likely be disappointed and the parent will most likely be frustrated by not being able to meet your expectations.

**Avoid feeling disloyal to one parent by loving another parent.**

Your parents' choice to dislike each other should not involve you. Your love for one parent does not mean that you are betraying the parent who does not share your feelings.

You have a right to love both your biological parents and stepparents, in spite of how they feel about each other.

## 34 — RECOMMENDED THINGS FOR STEPCHILDREN TO AVOID

**Avoid feeling unloved by your biological parent.**

The love that adults feel for each other is different from the love they feel for their children.

Your parents' love for another adult does not lessen or replace the love he or she has for you.

# RECOMMENDED THINGS FOR STEPCHILDREN TO AVOID

Avoid being around any stepfamily member who is unkind to you or who does not like you.

Sometimes, no matter how hard you try to get a person to like you, he or she does not. When this happens, you need to realize that something is most likely wrong with the other person, not with you.

It is not good to spend time with people who do not like you. Instead, you should try to spend time with people who do like you.

## 36 — RECOMMENDED THINGS FOR STEPCHILDREN TO DO

For stepchildren to make being part of a stepfamily a positive experience, it is necessary to do several things.

**Realize that your biological parent's decision to marry your stepparent does *not* mean that you must**
- love your stepparent,
- consider your stepparent a replacement for your biological parent who is not living with you,
- call your stepparent "Mom" or "Dad" or any other name you think should be reserved for a biological parent,
- give a stepparent any kind of physical affection that you do not want to give, or
- tell the stepparent anything you do not actually feel or believe is true.

FROM THE VERY BEGINNING MY DAD TOLD ME THAT MY STEPMOM WAS **NOT** MY MOM AND THAT I DIDN'T HAVE TO LOVE HER OR ACT AS IF I DID. SO, AT FIRST I HAD ALMOST NOTHING TO DO WITH HER.

# RECOMMENDED THINGS FOR STEPCHILDREN TO DO — 37

**Give yourself and the other members of your stepfamily time to adjust to the new situation.**

Strong feelings such as trust and love take time and work to develop. It should never be assumed that these things will happen immediately or automatically. In most cases it takes at least one year for people to develop a trust and love for each other. This is especially true of stepfamily members.

Remember, bad relationships can happen instantly, but good relationships take time to happen.

## 38 — RECOMMENDED THINGS FOR STEPCHILDREN TO DO

**Realize that because your stepparent shares the responsibility for you, he or she has the right to share in disciplining you.**

As an adult in the family, your stepparent will most likely be expected to assume some responsibility for you. He or she will be expected, at times, to do whatever is necessary to contribute to your survival and growth. In addition, your stepparent's life will be affected by your misfortunes, mistakes, and misbehavior. Because these things are true, your stepparent deserves to have some control over what you can and cannot do.

### RECOMMENDED THINGS FOR STEPCHILDREN TO DO — 39

Cooperate with whichever parent you are with even though each of your parents might have different ways of parenting.

There is no *one* correct way to be a parent. There are many ways to be a good parent. Every parent has a right to decide for himself or herself what kind of parent to be.

# 40 — RECOMMENDED THINGS FOR STEPCHILDREN TO DO

**Cooperate with the rules of whatever household you are in at the time.**

No two families are alike. Every family has its own set of rules and ways of doing things. Most likely, the families that you are a part of will be different from each other. This means that you will need to respond differently around each family you spend time with.

**RECOMMENDED THINGS FOR STEPCHILDREN TO DO — 41**

**Be a responsible member of your stepfamily.**

Be willing to do your share of the work that needs to be done around the house. Be supportive of the things other people in your stepfamily need or want to do.

## RECOMMENDED THINGS FOR STEPCHILDREN TO DO

**Treat the people in your stepfamily kindly and respectfully.**

Even though you do not have to love or show affection to the other members of your stepfamily, it is important that you treat them with kindness and respect.

No matter how you feel about the members of your stepfamily, they are human beings, and as such, they deserve to be treated with kindness and respect.

# RECOMMENDED THINGS FOR STEPCHILDREN TO DO — 43

**Communicate honestly and accurately with the people in your stepfamily.**

If you do not tell other stepfamily members what you truly think or feel, they might try to guess. If they guess incorrectly and act on what they think is true, they might do something that will displease you. Or they might *not* do something that you need or want them to do.

If you have a difficult time talking to stepfamily members, try writing a note or letter to them.

## RECOMMENDED THINGS FOR STEPCHILDREN TO DO

**Exercise your right to contribute to decisions that affect you.**

Some of these decisions might include
- what you will call your stepparent,
- what your last name will be,
- whether or not you will be adopted by your stepparent, and
- when and how you will stay in touch with the biological parent you do not live with.

If you feel that your thoughts are not being considered when these important decisions are being made, ask someone such as your teacher or school counselor to help you talk to your parents.

**RECOMMENDED THINGS FOR STEPCHILDREN TO DO — 45**

Maintain your own individuality even though you are part of an expanded family.
- Set aside special times that you can spend alone with your biological parents.
- Ask your parents to help you determine what space in the house can be exclusively yours (i.e., sleeping area, closet space, etc.). Then ask that these areas be "off limits" to everyone else in the family.
- Set aside times and places in and around your house where you can spend some private time alone.

## 46 — CONCLUSION

Living with a stepfamily can enhance and enrich your life.

## CONCLUSION — 47

Living with a stepfamily can cause you to grow and become a better person.

## 48 — CONCLUSION

Whether living with a stepfamily is good or bad for you depends a lot on what *you* do to make the experience positive or negative.

www.ingramcontent.com/pod-product-compliance
Lightning Source LLC
Chambersburg PA
CBHW081407070526
44583CB00020B/2718